P9-BZT-677

PICTURE BOOKS

Something to Tell the
GRANDCOWS

Written by Eileen Spinelli • Illustrated by Bill Slavin

Eerdmans Books for Young Readers

Grand Rapids, Michigan • Cambridge, U.K.

To my Russian friends, Felix and Olga and Liza and Rita and Masha and their families
—E. S.

For my sister, Ruth, who has had more adventures than anyone I know
—B. S.

Text © 2004 Eileen Spinelli
Illustrations © 2004 Bill Slavin

Published 2004 by Eerdmans Books for Young Readers
An imprint of Wm B Eerdmans Publishing Company
255 Jefferson S.E., Grand Rapids, Michigan 49503
P.O. Box 163, Cambridge CB3 9PU U.K.

All rights reserved
Manufactured in China

06 07 08 09 10   7 6 5 4

Library of Congress Cataloging-in-Publication Data
Spinelli, Eileen.
Something to tell the grandcows / written by Eileen Spinelli ; illustrated by Bill Slavin.
p. cm.
Summary: Hoping to have an adventure to impress her grandcows, Emmadine the cow joins Admiral Richard E.
Byrd on his 1933 expedition to the South Pole.
ISBN-10: 0-8028-5304-8 ISBN13: 978-0-8028-5304-2 (paper : alk. paper)
ISBN-10: 0-8028-5236-X ISBN13: 978-0-8028-5236-6 (hardcover : alk. paper)
[1. Cows-Fiction. 2. Antarctica-Discovery and exploration-Fiction. 3. South Pole-Fiction. 4. Grandparents-Fiction.
5. Byrd, Richard Evelyn, 1888-1957--Fiction.] I. Slavin, Bill, ill. II. Title.
PZ7.S7566Sq 2004
[E]--dc21
2003008824

The illustrations were created with acrylics on gessoed paper.
The type was set in GoudySans.
Art Director—Gayle Brown
Graphic Designer—Matthew Van Zomeren

SOUTH POLE

Little America

BYRD ANTARCTIC EXPEDITION
1933 · 1935

There were indeed several cows on one of Admiral Byrd's expeditions . . .

Farmer Fergus could tell his grandchildren about the time he wrestled an alligator at the Virginia State Fair.

Georgetta the pig could tell her grandpigs about the time she hot-air-ballooned across Mexico.

But what could Emmadine the cow tell her grandcows?

About the time she swatted seventeen horseflies?
Right.

Or the time she chased a crow from the corn?
Whoop-dee-doo.

So when Emmadine learned that Admiral
Richard E. Byrd was looking for a few good cows
to take to the South Pole, she volunteered.

It was October 1933 when Emmadine sailed off in a ship with two other cows (one red, one brown), 153 dogs, 56 explorers, and an assortment of boxes, barrels, snowshoes, skis, jelly, coffee, ukuleles, books, toothbrushes, and frying pans.

The crew waved their hats and grinned goodbye!

The dogs yapped.

The other cows dozed on beds of straw.

The ocean splashed merrily.

And Emmadine got seasick.

She moaned. She groaned. She wished she were back at the farm. But the ship was not about to turn back for one cow.

Week after week the old steamer pitched and tossed on the waves.

Then one day the sun glared silver-bright on an iceberg.

A crewman shouted, "Ice Ho!"

They had reached the South Pole.

Oh, wouldn't the grandcows be amazed!

Emmadine climbed into her warmest woolen socks. She wrapped a scarf round and round her neck. She put on the uddermuff that Georgetta the pig had knitted for her.

Then she made her way to the deck.

Here the air was white with swirling snow.

Emmadine watched as the crew drove anchors into the ice and ran planks down from the ship.

This was the coldest place on earth.

Emmadine's breath turned to ice crystals. Her teeth chattered like spoons. She wished she were home swatting horseflies.

The cowherd came. Carefully he guided Emmadine down the plank and onto the crusted snow.

While Emmadine waited for the crew to unload the ship, she saw velvety seals basking on ice cakes. She spotted a giant petrel grazing the sky. She sighted whales playing in the bay. Their foggy spouts echoed from the snow cliffs.

Oh, wouldn't the grandcows be amazed!

Emmadine noticed a penguin scooting on its stomach across the ice. It stopped smack in front of Emmadine. It stood up.

Emmadine, curious, leaned forward. She sniffed the penguin's shiny coat.

Not a good idea!

Swack! The penguin slapped Emmadine's nose with its flipper.

Before Emmadine could moo "ouch!" the penguin had waddled over to check out the dogs.

Emmadine sniffled. "I sure do miss Georgetta the pig."

But Georgetta was thousands of miles away.

At that moment the cowherd appeared with the other cows. He led all three, slip-sliding across the ice to a ramshackle shed.

"Home sweet home," said the cowherd. He spread straw for bedding. He checked the stove. He brought out the milk pails.

"Ah," thought Emmadine. "Milking time. And after that, bedtime. My first night's sleep at the South Pole."

She waited for the sun to go down. "This is the longest sunset I ever saw," she mused.

The sun seemed stuck in the sky. In fact, it never did go down. For it was summer in the South Pole, and that meant sun in the morning, sun in the afternoon, sun all night.

When the cowherd explained this, Emmadine exclaimed, "Imagine! Sunlight twenty-four hours a day!"

Oh, wouldn't the grandcows be amazed!

But the red cow flicked her tail nervously.

And the brown cow began bawling.

"There, there," said the cowherd, tacking a piece
of dark cloth to the window.

Then he picked up the ukulele that had been sitting in
the corner. Softly he played "Ukulele Lullaby."

Emmadine and the other cows soon fell fast asleep.

Emmadine dreamed she was chasing crows from the corn.

She woke at 6 A.M. to the sound of the wind, to the tinkling
of icicles. One icicle bonked her on the head.

If this was summer in the South Pole,
what would winter be like?

In time, Emmadine found out.

April 19 to be exact.

On that day the sky flared blue, green, red, and yellow. It was quite beautiful. Emmadine had never seen anything like it.

Oh, wouldn't the grandcows be amazed!

WESTCHESTER PUBLIC LIBRARY CHESTERTON, IN

Slowly the sun dropped below the horizon and stayed down.

Now it was darkness twenty-four hours a day.

This was more unsettling than light.

In the morning, the cowherd lit lanterns. He kept them lit until after supper.
But even cows can tell lanternlight from sunlight. It just wasn't the same.

Besides the darkness, winter at the South Pole brought fierce gales, deep,
dangerous drifts, hurling clouds of snow.

There was no leaving the shed for a
breath of fresh air or a bit of ski practice.

The red cow grew bored.

The brown cow grew moody.

So Emmadine decided to give dancing lessons.

She taught the red cow to tango.

She taught the brown cow to polka.

She even taught the cowherd to do
the hoochy-coochy.

Oh, wouldn't the grandcows be amazed!

Thinking about the grandcows, however, began to sadden Emmadine.

She was so far away.

Perhaps she would never see her grandcows again.

Perhaps she would have to stay at the South Pole forever.

She needn't have worried.

No one stays at the South Pole forever. One day when spring came, the cowherd led Emmadine out into the frosty air, across the ruffled snow, and onto the ship.

Emmadine could hardly believe it. She was going home.

When the ship finally reached homeport, there were crowds cheering. There were flags waving. There was a brass band playing.

Farmer Fergus met Emmadine at the dock.

So did the President of the United States.

He congratulated Emmadine. He presented her with a shiny gold medal. He kissed her on both cheeks.

Oh, wouldn't the grandcows be amazed!

About the President. About the iceberg and the whales and the sunlight and the darkness and the wind and the dancing and the whole South Pole adventure . . .

And of course they were.